I Wish That I Could Have a Pet

By Dorothy Rose • Pictures by Kelly Oechsli

A Wanderer Book Published by Simon & Schuster, Inc.

I wish that I could have a pet
to keep me company.

I'd care for him and teach him tricks
for all my friends to see.

You'd hear my fluffy KITTEN purr
if I could have my wish.

I'd fix a nice clean litter box
and feed him milk and fish.

To hear his song and watch him fly
a BIRD is what I need.

I'd clean his cage and keep it filled
with water, greens and seed.

If I could have a friendly DOG,
a puppy all my own,

I'd teach him how to sit and beg
and fetch his rubber bone.

If BUNNY was my furry pet
on greens and nuts he'd gnaw.

I'd build a little wooden hutch
and make a bed of straw.

My FISH would have a giant tank
complete with rocks and plants.

I'd feed them and I'd watch them swim
if I just had the chance.

One GERBIL would be fun to have,
or maybe I'd have two.

I'd gather tasty leaves and seeds
and sit and watch them chew.

A fuzzy little yellow CHICK
could move right in with me.

I'd feed him corn and keep him safe.
What fun a chick would be.

A HAMSTER is a gentle pet.
I've always wanted one.

I'd put a wheel inside his cage
for exercise and fun.

I'd love a PONY I could ride
who'd whinny, snort and neigh.

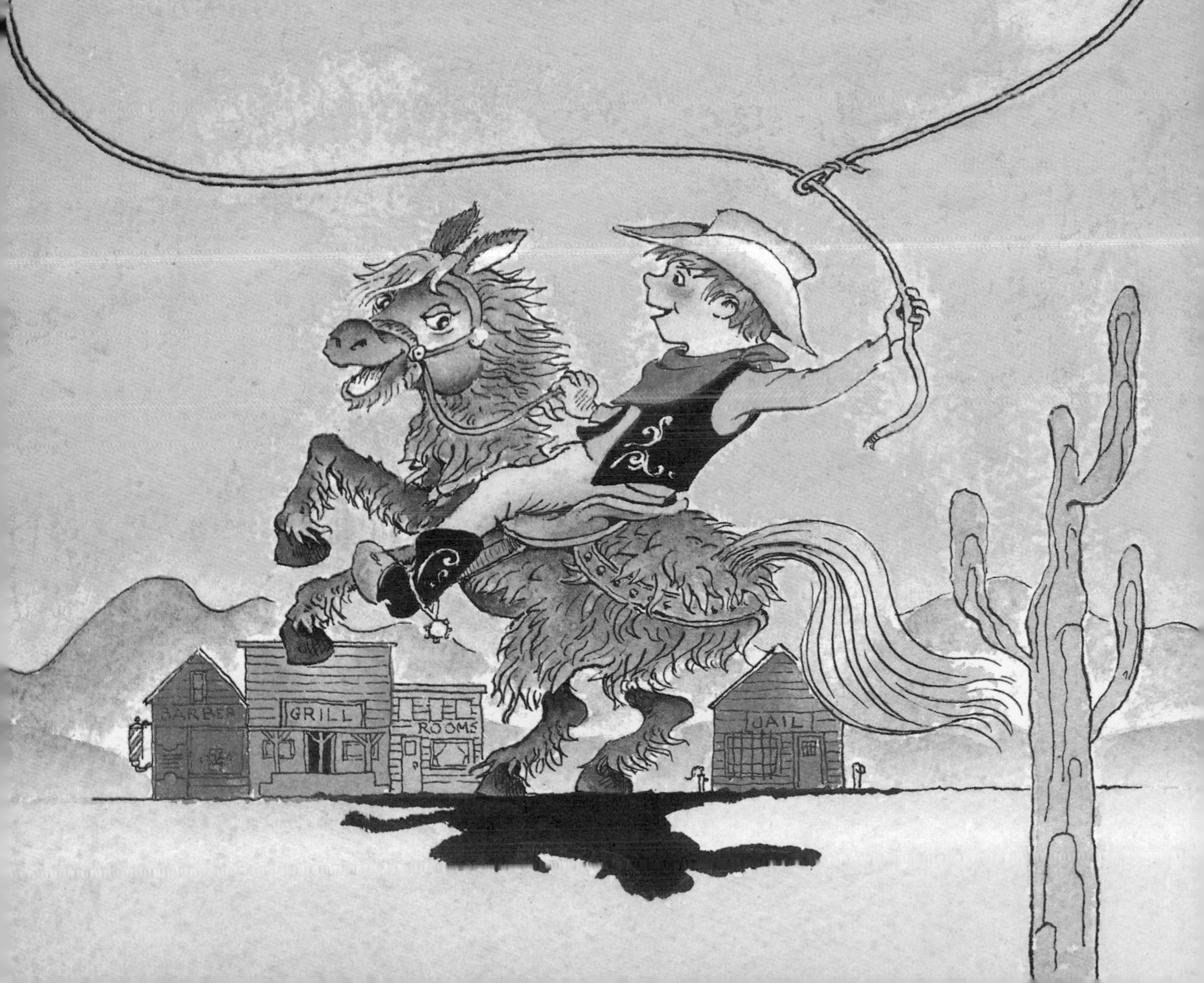

I'd groom him with a comb and brush
and feed him oats and hay.

I wish that I could have a pet.
Most any one would do.

And if by chance you feel the same,
I hope you get one, too.